AF493077

SUCCESSFUL SELF-PUBLISHING

HOW TO PUBLISH A BOOK WITHOUT A PUBLISHER

bloodsucking

- A 7-step guide to self-publishing on Amazon -

Kevin Albert

ISBN 978-9916-9940-2-3

Note: This work is derived from the author's experience in bookselling, writing, and publishing, and is meant to inform and inspire writers with tools and strategies for success in their own writing path. There is no single magic solution for everyone, and advice, wisdom, and insights should be carefully curated and adapted to suit each individual's needs, goals, and desires.

Suit up, because your personality isn't the first thing people see.

CONTENTS

A gift just for you!

Would you like to **read my next book completely FREE**? Scan the code below and **join my readers' club**!

Great surprises await you: be the first to read my new releases, listen to my audiobooks for free, get signed and personalized copies... and so much more!

Introduction

Having spent four long years writing my first book, in early 2016 I finally finished the last of dozens of corrections that my obsessive-compulsive disorder had forced me to subject my work to before considering it ready to see the light of day. My moment had finally come. Before I knew it, my book would be published.

At least, that's what I thought. But it wasn't until the middle of that year, some six months later, that the book finally went on sale. Is it really necessary for so much time to pass between finishing a book and seeing it published?

Well, THAT DEPENDS.

Let's look at two extreme scenarios: if you throw yourself at the mercy of a publishing house, your masterpiece may end up being published years after your death (it happened to J.R.R. Tolkien with *The Lord of the Rings*), but if you self-publish without taking care over the details, you can do it in under thirty minutes.

Neither of these two routes are very promising: the former because you will never enjoy the success your book may achieve, and the latter because your rush to get published without crossing the t's and dotting the i's is normally a guarantee you'll fail.

Is there a middle ground? Is it possible to publish a book without waiting months or years for a company to consider you worthy of publishing but to do it with the same guarantee of success?

Yes, THERE IS.

And that, my friend, is the aim of this book: I am going to show you how I went from publishing my first book in just over six months, to doing it in under a week and with **maximum chances of success**.

Self-publishing vs Publishing houses

If you already know me, or if you read the first part of *Successful Self-Publishing*, you'll know that I ended up self-publishing my first book – *Branding Secrets*[1] – through Amazon. Making this decision was what delayed the launch of my book by six long months, not the typical delays of a publishing company.

I'm someone who, when making an important decision, analyzes every possible variable. Of course, having dedicated over four years to writing my book, this was undoubtedly a fundamental decision, and not one I was

---

[1] *soykevinalbert.com/books/bs*

prepared to leave to chance. So, as usual, I did my homework.

Although I tend to begin my research online, I had become a real expert during my work on my first book, so I had close links with many other experts (in and out of the world of branding) who just "happened" to have one or more published books.

So, the first step in my investigation consisted of meeting with six of these experienced authors in order to ask them what route they had chosen to take (publishing house or doing it themselves) and how they had found it.

I don't know what surprised me more: discovering that they had all published their books through a company, or finding out their reasons for doing it. Five of them agreed that going through a publishing house "gives you more cachet".

If I wasn't disconcerted enough at these initial findings, the next discovery left me shellshocked: five of the six (yes, the same ones who said "cachet") **had paid to have their books published**. And not small change: some of them admitted to me that **publishing had involved a financial investment they would probably never recoup through book sales**.

WHAT THE HELL?! To get published, I had to get into debt?! That's not what happens in the movies!

I thought that if you wrote a good book and were "lucky" enough for a publishing house to like it and get behind it, they would take care of absolutely everything: give you a check and a percentage of the sales, and all you had to do was sign books in Barnes & Noble.

Either I was an idiot... or something strange was happening here.

And it turned out, something strange was happening.

Luckily for my research, one of these six experts had not had to pay to publish their work and could confirm to me that in fact, things worked very similarly to what I had thought (without the Barnes & Noble part). They explained to me, although their initial paycheck was for less than $2000 and their annual royalties close to zero, **a publishing house never asks you for money to publish your book.**

The other people I talked to had fallen for what's known as the "publishing scam". Roughly speaking, it consists of a **printing house**, which makes money by printing stuff, presenting themselves as a **publishing house**, which makes money by selling books. It doesn't matter if they call it **co-publishing** or **self-publishing** – if you have to pay *anything* to publish your book, IT'S A PRINTING HOUSE.

If you want to find out more about the topic, just google "publishing scam" and you can read all about these con artists. You'll find personal stories of rage and frustration that I hope will help stop you from falling into their **perfectly designed trap**.

Having got to this point, and with the information I had obtained, I had two options:

1. I could publish my book through a printing house in less than a month, spending a few thousand dollars[2].

2. I could spend months contacting "real" publishing houses and crossing my fingers that one would do me the "favor" of publishing my book and paying me two thousand measly dollars plus some practically non-existent royalties[3].

---

[2] The authors I spoke to spent between $5000 and $20,000.
[3] If you're a new writer, conditions will rarely be better than this.

Looking at this unencouraging panorama, all I could do was use my entrepreneurial spirit and discover the self-publishing route for myself.

As you can probably guess, the experiment went well. So well that not only did I finish writing the book you're holding now, but some of these authors, who were so happy with their "cachet", ended up being clients of mine :)

Reasons to self-publish

We've already looked at two good reasons to opt for self-publication:

1. It's much faster than doing it through a **real publishing house**.

2. It's much cheaper than doing it through a **fake publishing house**.

Maybe the question we should be asking ourselves is:

Why NOT self-publish?

If we went on the criteria of the writers I interviewed, there would be two main reasons for opting for a traditional publishing house:

1. Using a reputable publishing house **gives you more cachet**.

2. Self-publishing "professionally" **is not an easy task**.

To tell you the truth, I partially agree with them. Let me explain:

In terms of the first point, it's true that if you publish via an internationally renowned publishing house and it helps you to sell millions of copies worldwide, then yes, it gives you a certain cachet. Buuuut, if you pay several thousand dollars for the "co-publishing" place around the corner to "print" your book, I'm sorry to say that you're not an author with cachet, you're a *sucker*.

And when it comes to the second point, I agree once again. Self-publishing "professionally" is no mean feat. You only have to take a look at Amazon's catalog to see the aberrations that millions of indie authors upload to the platform showing off their Photoshop skills (or worse still, their Paint[4] skills!) or delighting readers with the wonders of Word's autocorrect. To tell you the truth, when I say I'm a self-published writer, I'm afraid people will associate me with these phenomena.

But what would you say if I told you you could self-publish your book with the same quality as a publishing house, but without having to learn graphic design or get a degree in philology – and that you could do it in less than a week?

Self-publishing a book is easy. As I said before, you can do it in under thirty minutes. Self-publishing a book **without it looking self-published** is a little trickier, but that's exactly what this book is for!

---

[4] Microsoft Paint is a simple raster graphics editor that has been included with all versions of Microsoft Windows.

If you follow the steps I'm going to give you in this guide, not only will you be able to self-publish with the same quality as a good publishing house – and achieve the same cachet or even more – you'll enjoy many of the hidden benefits that we self-published authors can obtain. These include the freedom to write what you want in your own words, not what your editor decides is more "suitable", and the control and flexibility to experiment and try new things when you – and you alone – decide, earning some good money along the way.

If all these reasons haven't convinced you and you still think you should go through a good publishing house, go ahead – but I advise you first to explore what you might achieve with "simple" self-publication. Once you've demonstrated that there are thousands of people prepared to buy your book, contact that company you're so interested in. This way, it will be you who negotiates the conditions.

Why Amazon?

If you've read everything I've said and become an unconditional fan of the idea of publishing yourself, like I am, then you might be wondering:

Where do I publish my book?

There are many platforms you can self-publish on – some even have better conditions than Amazon (in terms of royalties). So why did I ultimately decide on Amazon, and why do I not hesitate in advising you to do the same?

There are several reasons that tipped the scales for me in favor of Bezos's[5] company, but there is one so blatant that it requires little

---

[5] Jeff Preston Bezos is Amazon's founder and CEO.

explanation: Amazon is the world's biggest bookshop, so **it has the biggest database possible of readers for your book**. This means that **the potential for selling and earning money with your work is much greater on Amazon** than on any other platform.

And if that's not enough: it also has the best control panel where you can closely follow everything that happens with your book, an exclusive platform where you can promote it, the option to publish both digital and physical books in dozens of different formats, an unparalleled delivery service (you'll quickly see your book delivered by smart drones in just a few hours or minutes), and more.

Okay, okay, so Amazon is the sh*t – but why not publish on the other platforms, too? I was mulling over this question for months. I eventually decided to postpone the idea indefinitely. There were two reasons why I made this decision:

1. Publishing on a platform requires just a few minutes, but **mastering a platform requires dedication**, so I ended up realizing it would be better to focus my energies on the n°1 platform, rather than spreading myself thin over others with less potential.

2. **With Amazon, exclusivity is rewarded**. If you promise not to publish your eBook anywhere else, Amazon offers you the chance to participate in its KDP Select program.

And this, my friends, is where it gets interesting.

The KDP Select Program

KDP Select is a marketing program that involves giving Amazon exclusive rights to sell your book in digital format (you can still sell hard copies or audio versions wherever you want) for 90 days. At the end of this period, you can decide whether to continue with the program or not.

This option **is not selected** by default, so you have to check it when you publish. If you don't do it right then, you can sign up later from your book's homepage. It also renews automatically, so if you want to leave, you need to uncheck the option before the 90 days are up.

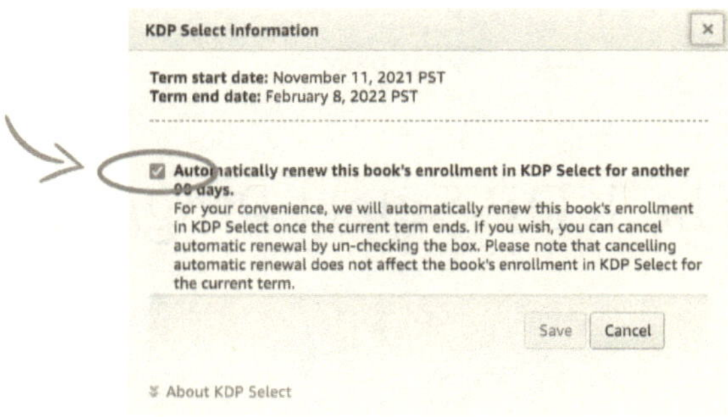

Where to find the KDP Select option.

Signing up to this program gives you a series of very interesting benefits and tools to help you succeed with your book – and Amazon is expanding and improving them all the time.

Using and analyzing these tools isn't something to worry about too much yet[6], since it's more about the marketing stage, but I do think you should know **the 3 main benefits of KDP Select** when you are publishing your book and deciding whether or not to give Amazon that exclusivity:

---

[6] If you're curious, you can find out more on their own website: *soykevinalbert.com/kdpselect*

1. **Better commission.** The first advantage of signing up to this program is that, in countries such as Japan, India, Mexico and Brazil, your royalties from sales of your eBook will go from **35% to 70%**.

2. **More income.** Every book registered with KDP Select is automatically included in **Kindle Unlimited**, a program with which customers can read as many books as they like and keep them indefinitely in return for a monthly subscription. For you as a writer, this opens up **a new income stream** since in addition to receiving royalties on the sales of your book, **Amazon will also pay you for every page read** by a Kindle Unlimited customer.

3. **Greater visibility.** The evidence seems to suggest that Amazon gives "better treatment" – that is, more visibility – to KDP Select books. In addition, the pages

read – alongside sales – will improve a book's ranking and see it climb the ladder in Amazon's library, which gives it even more visibility. It's a wonderful virtuous cycle: **more visibility, more sales; more sales, more visibility**.

STEP 1

Editing:
Professional proofreading at affordable prices

Once you have decided to self-publish your book, whether with Amazon or another platform, it's all hands on deck.

Although I consider editing to be more a part of the writing process than the publishing one, I decided to include this chapter for those who skipped the first book in the series: *Successful Self-Publishing: How to write a non-fiction book in 30 days*[7]. If you already read it, skip to the next

---

[7] *soykevinalbert.com/books/ssp1*

chapter. If not, and your book has not been edited yet – or even if it has – this chapter is going to do you a lot of favors.

Whether you're a pretty casual writer (like me) and are working with a draft, or you consider yourself the next Dickens with a new and improved *Great Expectations* ready for the bookshelf, **your book must go through the process of being edited before it can be published**. Period.

During this process, your work will pass through three sets of hands: yours, your beta readers', and those of a professional editor.

Stage 1: self-editing.

The first check of your book is up to you. And it will be a triple check: rather than reading your book and trying to correct it all in one go, you will read it three times, paying attention to a single aspect on each reading. If you try to fix it all in one step, you'll find it an uphill struggle and feel like you're not making progress (and you may not be).

1. For the **first check**, all you do is **underline and take notes** of any mistakes or inconsistencies you find, as well as any improvements or fixes you'd like to make.

2. For the **second**, you should pay attention to the **coherency and fluidity** of your text, reorganizing sections and even adding or removing sections as you see fit.

3. For the **third and final check**, all you have to do is go over the **spelling and grammar** mistakes.

And that's it – your book is ready for the next stage. Don't keep checking it endlessly: this is one of the biggest mistakes a writer can make. It's better to have a complete but imperfect book than one "perfect" chapter of an incomplete book.

Don't forget: finished is better than perfect.

Stage 2: beta readers.

If two heads are better than one, imagine what twenty can do. Beta readers are a fantastic way to get feedback during the editing of your book: finding inconsistencies and grammatical mistakes in the text, giving you an idea of how your book will be received by future readers, and so on.

A beta reader is basically anyone who reads your draft and gives you constructive criticism on it (something more than "I liked it" or "I didn't". You benefit from their corrections and suggestions, and they get a free copy of your book's draft.

Your close friends and relatives are not the best beta readers, as it's hard for them to be objective; they will be trying not to hurt your feelings. That's not what you need right now.

Once you have chosen your beta readers, be sure to send them some brief indications of what you're expecting of them along with a digital copy of your manuscript. This could be simply underlining the grammatical mistakes they find or a short list of specific questions on your book's content.

What should you look for in the feedback you receive? The comments you get from your beta readers don't mean you have to modify your book in accordance with every suggestion they make. Trying to please everyone is impossible – in fact, it's a mistake. **What you're looking for are common points.** Find the suggestions that keep coming up, and decide if you need to make some final alterations before moving on to the third stage.

Stage 3: your professional editor.

You're nearly there. It's time for the third and final stage of editing of your manuscript, where you will turn that chaotic draft you were checking just a few days ago into a real work of art.

Your book has not been through three self-edits and your beta readers, and you may be tempted to skip this final step and save a few bucks. Don't make that mistake.

There are certain limitations to your self-editing and your beta readers' suggestions, so having a professional editor go into depth on your work is **a very important step that you can't miss out before hitting the "publish" button**.

A good editor will help you polish your draft, soften any little (or not so little) faux pas, and offer you some suggestions on how to improve your book. Finding a professional editor is easy – doing it on a budget, not so much.

Of all the places you can look for an editor for your book, I recommend _Upwork_[8], a virtual marketplace that puts the best freelancers from around the world in touch with companies or individuals looking for talented professionals.

Basically, all you have to do is sign up to the platform and publish your job offer (editing your book) following the steps indicated. You will start receiving proposals from dozens of freelancers interested in editing your book. Your only job is to find the professional who offers you the best quality at the best price.

How to choose your editor.

The best thing about working with a platform like Upwork is that you can check the profiles of

[8] upwork.com

all the freelancers who offer to edit your book: their rates, education, portfolio – and, most important of all, their reviews.

You can really get lost among so much information and spend days checking profiles. But you don't need to. This is how I do it:

First, I discard all proposals from freelancers who have earned less than $12,000 on the platform and who don't have at least a 90% customer satisfaction rate. Just by doing this, you will be shortlisting just a few proposals. From the professionals still standing, you can do a little survey and find out if any of them specialize in, or have previously edited, books on the same topic as yours, and mark these as favorites.

Once you've reached this point, all that's left is to discuss prices.

How much does it cost to edit a book through Upwork?

The answer is simple: **however much you want to spend**.

It's been years now that I use Upwork for something at least once a week (you can't imagine the kinds of things you can commission). The first thing I learned about working with these kinds of platforms is that, just like in the offline world, prices vary to infinity and beyond.

For the same book (let's say, thirty thousand words), edited by two freelancers with the same degree of training and experience, you can expect to pay anything from $100 to over $5000.

The official prices for editing a book are normally between $0.005 and $0.015 per word. I say "official" because those are the recommendations of the *Editorial Freelancers Association.* But that doesn't mean you can't find much higher or much lower rates with similar results. This **abysmal** difference is due to several factors: the main one is the freelancer's country of origin, since living costs are different in Spain and in the US, for example. But it also depends on how in-demand or "famous" the freelancer is.

But don't get downhearted – this is the magic of these marketplaces. Remember: if the professional has at least 90% customer satisfaction and has earned at least $12,000 on the platform, you can more or less guarantee they will do a good job.

To help guide you a little, for my last books – between fifteen and thirty thousand words each – I have paid an average of $80.

Layout:
It's not enough to be an expert, you have to look like one

Once your book has been through the editing process, you might think your manuscript is ready for publication. Wrong. What you say (your draft) and how you say it (your edited book) are equally important as the way you present it: that is, your book's layout.

This may seem superficial, and you might think all that matters to how your book is received is the content itself. I'm happy to tell you that this is not the case. Form matters – a lot!

And I say I'm happy because layout is one of the simplest steps in the creation process, despite being the one lots of self-published authors skip out.

This is a great opportunity for writers to take things seriously, because even with a lower quality of content, your book will be better rated (get more stars) by readers, which will make it climb the ranks on Amazon, be more visible and get more sales than other books from the competition who didn't pay enough attention to this simple process.

What is layout?

Layout is the distribution of the elements of a given space on the page – in other words, the process of giving form to the book and getting it ready to be published.

During this process, you should pay attention to aspects such as margins, typography, line and paragraph spacing, style of titles and subtitles, page headers and footers, and so on.

Your aim with your layout is to give form coherence to the whole text: to choose a style and guarantee that it will be applied correctly throughout the entire book, so that the final result is conducive to comprehension and to make the experience as pleasant as possible for your readers.

Whose job is layout?

In general, if there are professionals specializing in a certain task – like there are for layout – I recommend outsourcing it. This is because if people do this task for a living, then no matter how simple it may seem to us, it must be trickier than it looks – and I'm not going to recommend that you learn a new profession just in order to do something you might never need to do again in your life.

However, given that layout is a process that you need to go through several times in order to correct mistakes you find after your book has been published, as well as updating sections or expanding on the content, we're going to look at two options: outsourcing via Upwork, or DIY. This way, you can choose the option that adapts to your personal preferences and your particular situation.

1. Outsourcing: Upwork.

Just like you did when looking for an editor, all you have to do is publish your job offer (your book layout) following the steps indicated by the platform.

Disregard offers from less experienced professionals (those who have earned less than

$12,000), as well as those with a success rate under 90%.

From the professionals still standing, look for those offering a reasonable rate (around $85 for either a physical or a digital version of your book) and prepared to help you with later corrections without charging you for the whole job again. This is an important point: if the freelancer you hire doesn't cover later modifications, or simply disappears from the platform, you will have to pay for the whole layout again. It happened to me, which is why, in this case, I broke my own rules and decided to learn to do it myself.

2. Do it yourself.

If you decide to DIY it, you'll need just two things: a Word template, and a little patience.

For the first of these, I recommend taking a look at Book Design Templates, a website specializing in book templates with over fifty different designs and prices varying between $29 and $59 per individual license:

soykevinalbert.com/bookdesigntemplates

All their templates are ready for editing, both in physical and in digital format. They also have some great tutorials to help you learn to do it easily, even if your Word knowledge is scant.

Cover:
Like it or not, your book will be judged by its cover

Yes, as I explained in the first instalment of *Successful Self-Publishing*, while your title is your n°1 secret to being **discovered** among the millions of books available on Amazon, without a doubt, your cover is the n°1 secret to being **chosen** from them.

Given that the cover is going to play such an important role in your book's success, **you need to take it seriously**. By this, I mean that you're not going to design it yourself, nor your brother-in-law who's great at drawing, nor your cousin with a degree in art... nor anyone who isn't a professional at designing book covers!

This part is important. In order to ensure we get a good book cover (one that sells), not only are we going to hire a professional in graphic design... **we're going to hire hundreds!**

Designer tournaments.

I really love tournaments and competitions, since I think they're a great way to get people to give it their all. That's why, in order to get the best cover possible for your book, you're going to pit dozens – or hundreds – of graphic designers against each other. To do this, you're going to use the platform Freelancer – although I personally don't like it as much as Upwork, it allows you to create contests or tournaments.

Why a contest?

Normally, to choose the best freelancer to work with, I recommend an active search like the ones I recommended performing through Upwork. However, on this occasion, in addition to looking for the best freelancer, **you're looking for ideas** – and the more, the merrier.

Paying a **good professional** $50 and asking them to suggest a hundred different ideas for your book cover is not realistic, no matter how cheap the cost of living is in their country. But you *can* ask for a different proposal from each of a hundred freelancers, and award a single $50 prize to the winning candidate.

How to create a contest.

Preparing a contest on Freelancer is easy. Go to the website *freelancer.com* and click "post a project" in the top right corner. Describe your project and indicate the skills that the participating freelancers will need to have (examples include graphic design, illustration, or Photoshop). Next, it will ask you how you want to create the job: either "post a project" or "start a contest". Once you have selected "start a contest", set your budget, how many days you want the competition to last, and whether you want the prize to be guaranteed[9].

To give you an idea of this, for the cover of this book – well, three of them – I set a $60 budget, allowed seven days for participation, and chose to guarantee the prize. With this configuration, I received 123 different pitches: many of them with a completely different design for each of the three volumes of the *Successful Self-Publishing* series. This means that each cover cost me a little over twenty dollars.

To increase your chances of getting the "perfect" book cover, one that you love, it's

---

[9] This means that you guarantee that even if no proposal really grabs you, you will choose one to award the prize to.

essential that you guide the participants in your contest. They need to know what you're looking for. This, along with a highly detailed description of the project, can be achieved with the following two tips:

1. Before posting your contest, do a search for covers on Amazon and Google and bookmark any that you really like. Choose book covers that are unrelated as well as related to your field. Once you have a good few (at least twenty), look for similarities between them. What is it that caught your eye? Why did you decide to bookmark them? You might realize that all books in your genre use the same color scheme, that you find minimalistic designs appealing, that you prefer those with illustrations, or something else.

   When you upload your offer to Freelancer, include three to five of your favorite covers and indicate what you like best about them. Don't forget to specify that the final design needs to include a spine and back cover.

2. Check on your contest at least once a day and assign points to each proposal you receive. It's very important, if there's a cover you like much more than the others, that it has a higher points value than the others. If you have ten completely different proposals with the same points value, new candidates won't know what it was you liked or which elements to focus on in their designs. When it's clear that there is one idea you like more than the other, all participants will base themselves on that, trying to improve it. Similarly, if you haven't yet received one that grabs you, try not to award any of the designs five stars. This will ensure you keep receiving completely original pitches.

Prepare a survey.

As if the chance to create a contest wasn't already a little brutal, once the timeframe you set is up, you have the option to automatically schedule a survey so that your friends and acquaintances can help you choose the winning pitch.

This option is really interesting, and I recommend you always switch it on, even when you're clear on which design you like best. Imagine, for example, that you launch your survey and the proposal you had in mind gets almost no votes, while there's another one that it seems everyone loves. Wouldn't it make you reconsider? Remember that you're designing your cover to increase your book's chances of being chosen from Amazon's enormous online catalog, so if a significant proportion of people like the same proposal, surely it's at least worth considering.

Before you launch your survey, you need to wait for the timeframe you set to be up. Once the contest closes, you have up to four weeks to choose the winning proposal.

It's easy to create and share your survey. The platform will give you the option to select up to eight different pitches (or fewer, if you prefer). When you've selected the designs you want to include, Freelancer will give you some options for sharing them. I recommend you use the option to email your family and friends directly, as well as sharing a link to the survey on your social media. Once you've done this, wait five to seven days – and no longer – before looking over the results and making your final decision.

When you've chosen the winning proposal, you can award the prize to the design's creator – and, if necessary, ask them for a few adjustments or modifications before they deliver the finished product.

It's very important that you ensure the freelancer gives you the cover in an **editable format**, such as Photoshop or InDesign. This way, if you need to make any changes to the design in the future, any designer can help you to update it. In addition, you'll receive an **intellectual property contract** that guarantees that the work belongs to you.

And you're done!

If you've followed my steps, then in under fifteen days and for a measly $50, you can have a great book cover in your hands: designed by a professional, validated through a survey, and belonging completely to you. You're welcome.

Pro tip 1: To save time and unnecessary expenses adapting your cover to the final size of your book, upload the template Amazon gives you when you create your contest (along with the designs you include in your offer).

To get this template, go to: *kdp.amazon.com/cover-templates*, choose the same size you used for the book's layout, enter the number of pages in your document, select the paper color (white, cream or colored) and click "download cover template".

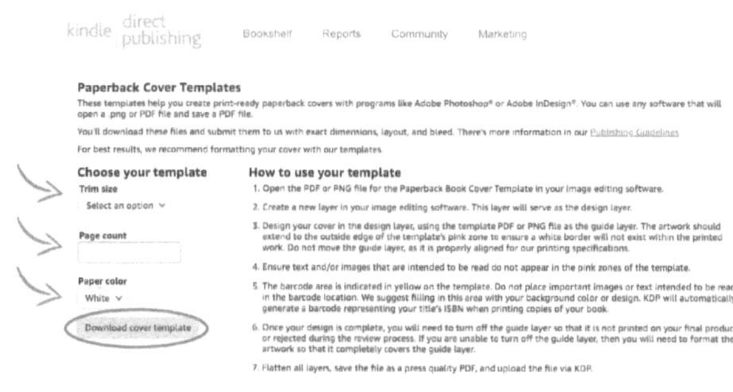

What you need to fill in to download your cover template.

Pro tip 2: For more objectivity in the results of your survey, before you choose the proposals you include in it, ensure they all have the same format: as simple as possible. Ideally, this will be a 2D design without additional decoration. If some of the designs you want to include in your survey were submitted in 3D or are simulated on top of a pretty desk or similar background, ask the creators to re-upload them in a simple format.

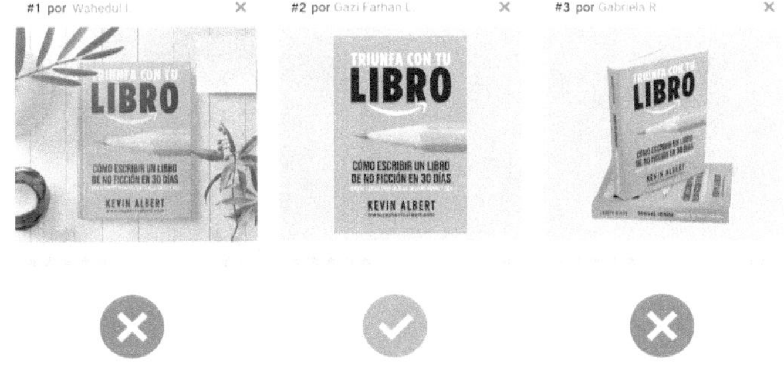

Left to right: design with decorations, 2D design, and 3D design.

S T E P   4

Description:
Your best sales letter

If you've managed to get potential readers to find your book, thanks to its title, and show an interest in it – thanks to its cover design – then it's time to sell it to them.

To do this, you're going to use a tool that's available to all authors on Amazon but that not many know how to make the most of: your book's description.

When we go to a bookshop in search of a new book and see one that catches our eye, what's the first thing we do? We turn it over and read the back cover. On Amazon, this is the role played by the description.

The mission of the description.

Since you can't be present each and every time someone is interested in your book in order to explain to them why they should choose you over the competition, it falls to your description to convince them. That is, it should play the role of a good commercial or sales letter.

How to write a perfectly irresistible description.

To write an irresistible description that's as appealing to Amazon itself as it is to your potential readers, you need just two things: using some simple copywriting skills (or persuasive writing), and applying a nice structure using HTML.

A) Copywriting.

Your book's description is not just there to tell the reader what the book is about (although that too). It's there to **persuade them to buy it**.

To achieve this, we're going to stick to 5 basic rules of copywriting:

1. **Emotion.**

In a non-fiction book, I consider that one of the best ways to start a description is by touching on your readers' sore points: that is, the problems they're facing, especially if you do so in question form.

For example, a good way of beginning the description for this book could be:

Have you spent years writing your book only to find no publishing house will touch it?

In addition, these first few words will be visible as soon as someone accesses the Amazon page for your book, without them needing to click on "read more" or scroll down. **Use them wisely**.

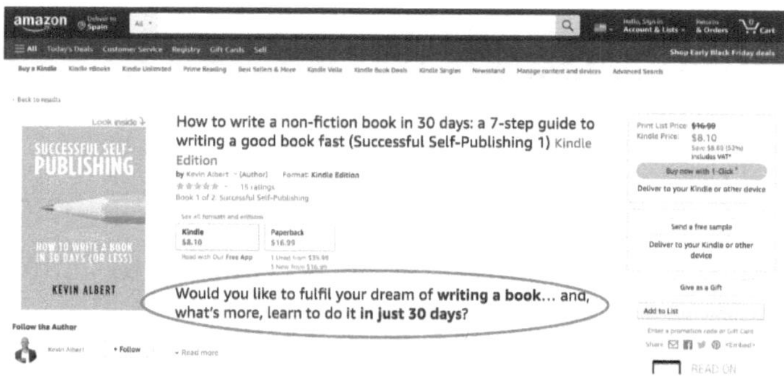

Visible part of the description on your book's product page.

2. Authority.

People look for others to trust in and follow their example. If you don't manage to portray yourself as an expert and/or to generate empathy with your readers, you're unlikely to sell your book.

Explain to the reader who you are to write this book. Why should they trust you? You may have a degree, a masters, a doctorate, you may have helped dozens or hundreds of people... or you may "simply" have been in their shoes and overcome the situation successfully.

3. Social proof.

Telling your readers why you're the best is all well and good, but if other people say it too, your credibility will shoot through the roof.

Specifically, being able to read what other customers of a book or other product think is one of the things that made Amazon the giant it is today. So, if you have a review from someone who's read your book, you can include it in your description.

If you don't have one yet, or if you receive new and/or better Amazon reviews, you can come back later and edit your description to add them or change the ones you included previously. Between three and five reviews in your description is more than enough.

You don't need to copy and paste the whole review: just write a summary or a standout phrase with the name of the person who wrote it. The more well-known they are, the more power their comments will have.

For example, I love to include my former teacher and fellow writer, José María Aznar, whenever I can. It's purely coincidental that he has the same name as the former prime minister of Spain… but people don't know that ;)

4. Benefits.

When a reader searches in the non-fiction section, they are normally trying to find a solution to a specific problem they have. Relieving that pain will be the main reason that will drive a user to buy your book – not necessarily your literary skills.

This means the benefits of your book can be the solution to your readers' problems. The reader must be able to see at a glance what benefits they will obtain from reading your book, so I recommend that you present them in a numbered list or with bullet points.

5. Call to action.

As I said before, you should view your description as a sales letter. As such, you should end it with a call to action, or CTA.

You need to finish your description with a phrase that tells the reader what they need to do after reading the description – that is, buy your book:

Stop talking about what you're going to do one day... AND JUST DO IT!

This is a great moment to touch on a sore point again:

If you let this chance go by, in a year's time you'll be regretting what you could have done and didn't.

Or add "urgency", another very potent copywriting resource, as long as it's true:

Don't hesitate! Introductory price ends this week.

Put your writing skills to work, and remember: don't sell, make them buy.

B) HTML.

Now that you have a perfectly optimized description thanks to some simple persuasive writing, it's time to dress it up. For this, we'll use HTML code, the language used on websites to format texts (among other things).

Why do this? Take a look.

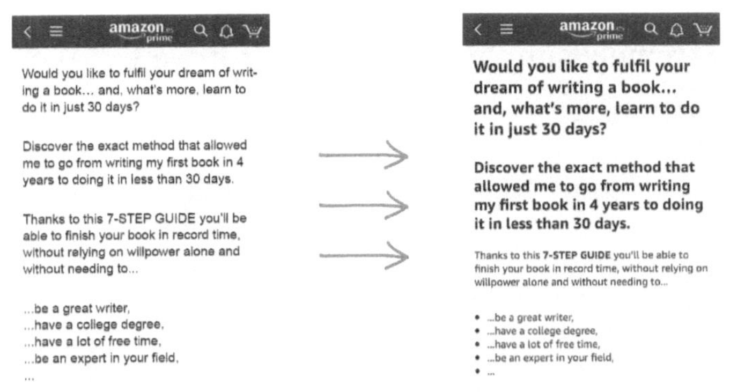

Description in plain text (left) and HTML (right).

As you can see, HTML enables you to change the size of the text, bold it, create lists with bullet points, and so on. All of this translates into better retention and better comprehension by your readers, which will undoubtedly have a positive effect on your sales.

And best of all is that you can do this without needing to learn absolutely anything about HTML coding, since while it was necessary for a long time to use external software to format descriptions, KDP finally decided to integrate this option and now we can do it directly from the extremely simple platform, as if it were a Word document:

You now have an irresistible description that I'm sure will attract views... and sales!

Want more sales? Let's look at how to get them.

Keywords:
How to ~~be found~~ get sold

Whether you're an established writer or about to launch your first book, keywords are a fundamental aspect of your book's marketing strategy.

The **correct use** of keywords on Amazon will help your book be found and **bought** by hundreds of thousands of readers around the world. If you have, or are planning to write, an amazing book but don't know how to get Amazon to show it to the **right readers**, then keywords will be your best allies.

What are keywords?

When someone decides to buy a new book on Amazon, they go onto the website and type what they're looking for into the search bar. Amazon uses the characters the person typed to decide what books to show them. The words or phrases the person search are known as *keywords*.

How to find LUCRATIVE keywords.

Now you know what keywords are and why they're so important, but before you start choosing the best keywords for your book, first you need to know what makes a keyword **lucrative** – because being found isn't the same as selling.

For a keyword to be lucrative, it needs to fulfil 3 requirements:

1. Enough searches.
2. Not too much competition.
3. Readers prepared to pay for it!

1. How to find keywords with enough searches.

In order for your book to be discovered by the right readers, you need to know what terms your readers use when searching on Amazon. To achieve this, the first thing you need to do is put yourself in the shoes of your potential readers, and make a list of the terms you think they might use to search for your book. These are usually words or phrases associated with the topic of your work, solutions you're bringing, or results they'll obtain if they put into practice what they learn from your book.

For example, for the book you're reading right now, a key term related to the topic could be "publishing on Amazon" or "self-publishing on

Amazon", while less obvious ones relating to the possible benefits they will obtain from reading it could be "passive income" or "extra money".

Once you have written this first list of keywords that you **think** your potential readers might use to find you, you need to **check** them.

To make sure your list is correct, use the **Amazon search bar** and start **slowly** typing each of the keywords or phrases you noted down. You need to type the characters one by one to see if Amazon suggests the term you were going to write before you finish writing it. If it does, that means that a significant number of people do, in fact, use these same words when searching.

To carry on with this example, let's imagine you thought that "publishing on Amazon" could be a good key phrase, so you go to the search bar and start typing the characters slowly. What would happen? As you can see in the below image, when you're up to "publishi...", Amazon will give you several suggestions relating to the keyword you were going to write.

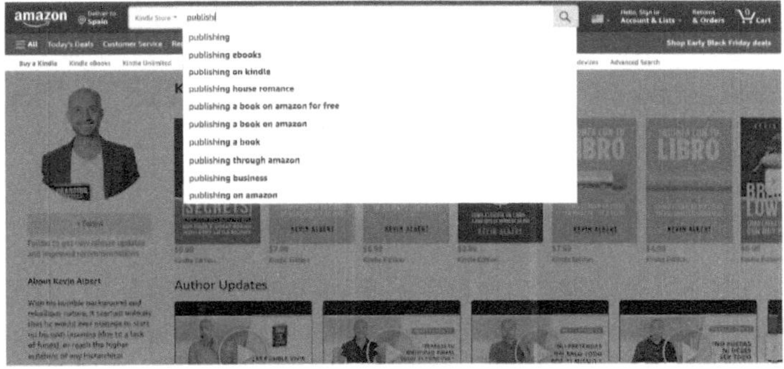

Amazon's predictive search function.

What conclusions can you draw from this? Firstly, that "publishing on Amazon" is indeed a key phrase that a significant number of people search for on Amazon – if it weren't, it wouldn't suggest it to us. And secondly, that "publishing a book" has more searches.

Amazon doesn't tell you how many people searched for a given word, but it does order the results by number of searches. This means that before you analyze both keywords in depth, it looks like "publishing a book" is a better option (with more searches) than "publishing on Amazon". But as they both appeared as suggestions, note them both down on your list for the second part of the analysis.

If any of the words you wrote down don't appear as suggestions when you start typing them into Amazon, you can deduce that they don't get many searches and discard them.

Things to bear in mind:

1. Make sure you're using your browser's incognito mode; if you don't, the results will be affected by your previous searches and they won't be reliable.

   To do this, just open the application bar in the browser you're using (Safari, Chrome, Firefox, or others) and select "New incognito [or private] window".

2. Select "Kindle Store" in Amazon's search bar before beginning your research. You're interested in finding out which words are popular in your section (books or eBooks), not on all of Amazon. By default, it will be set to "All Departments".

Search bar set to Kindle Store.

3. Do your research in the specific marketplace you're interested in (.com, .uk, .es, etc.), since these are different markets and their suggested terms may vary.

Tip: once you've chosen your keywords or phrases, type them into Amazon again and add one letter of the alphabet at a time. Start with A and work your way through to Z.

Example:

- Publishing on Amazon a
- Publishing on Amazon b
- Publishing on Amazon c
- Etc.

Look at the suggestions Amazon gives you. See anything good?

This is a great way to find some good (and lucrative) keywords that might never have occurred to you otherwise. In addition, if Amazon suggests them to you, it means they get a significant volume of searches.

2. How to know which keywords have the least competition.

Knowing which keywords are the most searched-for is very important, but not if you don't know the competition you face for each of them, you'll be making decisions blind.

Luckily, there is a very simple strategy you can use to ascertain the level of competition. All you have to do, while following the considerations I mentioned above, is type your key terms into Amazon's search bar and note down how many results you get.

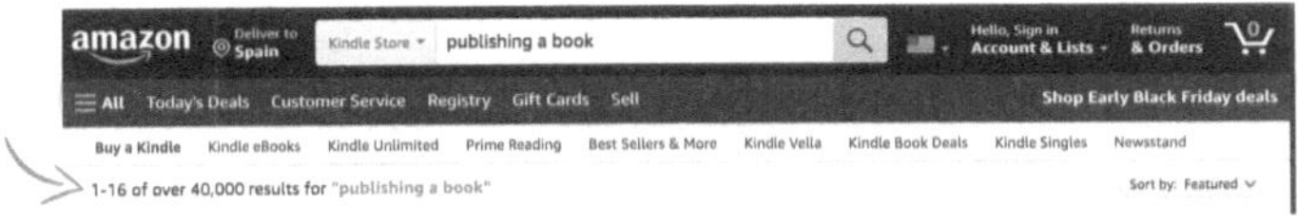

Number of results for the search term "publishing a book".

If you compare the two keywords in the previous point, you get the following results:

- Publishing a book: 40,000 results.
- Publishing on Amazon: 60,000 results.

Just by using this rudimentary system, we've discovered that "publishing a book", not only has more searches than our original key term ("publishing on Amazon"), but it also has less competition. *BOOM!*

You now have a list of keywords with a significant number of searches and you've ordered them according to their levels of competition. All that's left is to figure out which keywords have the most potential to generate sales.

3. How to find keywords readers will pay for.

Now we know which keywords from our list are most searched by readers, and which have less competition. Fantastic. But what use is this if it doesn't translate into sales?

This step is the most labor-intensive, but it's simple and undoubtedly the most important. To find out the sales potential of a keyword:

a) Type it into Amazon's search bar, bearing in mind the aforementioned considerations.

b) Note down the position in Amazon's ranking of the first ten books your search brings up. To find this position, you need to click on the book in question and scroll down to "product details". Here, you'll see the ranking for that book in its specific categories and in the **general classification of Amazon's bestsellers, or ABSR**[10]. This last figure is the one we're looking for.

---

[10] Amazon Bestseller Rank.

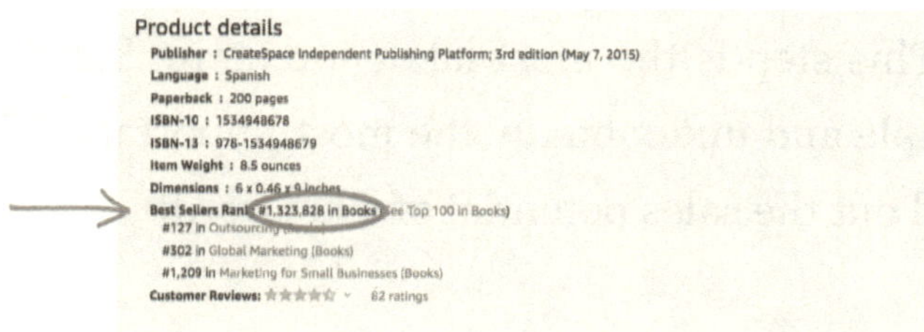

Where to find the general classification of bestsellers on Amazon.

c) Add up the positions of these books, and divide the resulting number by 10.

Compare this result for the different keywords you're analyzing. Those with a lower number will have less sales potential.

Pro tip: if you want to make this process more efficient and you're interested in knowing, among other things, how much your competition earns from their books (I'm nosy like that), I highly recommend the tool Publisher Rocket:

soykevinalbert.com/rocket

So, you have your lucrative keywords. Now what?

Now, it's time to use these keywords to show Amazon that your book deserves to be shown to your potential readers when they search... and when they don't!

To do this, try to include them, **without sounding robotic**, in your book's title and/or subtitle, in its description, and – of course – in the section reserved specifically for keywords.

When you're uploading your book to KDP, you'll find a space where you can enter up to seven keywords. If you did your homework properly, this section has tremendous value potential. Don't squander it.

Categories: Improve your ranking and sell more books

The categories you choose for your book when you upload it to KDP will have a direct impact on its potential to turn you into a bestselling author. There's no easier way to make your book a super-seller than by choosing your categories carefully. Similarly, if you choose the wrong categories, your chances of achieving this may vanish completely.

In the Amazon universe, it's much better to be a big fish in a little pond than a small fish in the

Pacific. The good news is that Amazon's algorithm, once you've conquered the small pond, will push you into the Pacific, too.

How important is it to be an Amazon bestseller?

Being an Amazon bestseller is not just an ego thing – it will **help you sell more books**. There are several factors that make this possible:

- **Amazon's algorithm itself** will give your book more exposure purely because it occupies the upper positions in a category.

- **Searches by category** by many readers will enable your book to be discovered by people who would not have otherwise found you.

- The **bestseller badge** Amazon will automatically add to your book listing once you have reached top position in a category will increase your views-to-sales conversion ratio. In other words, for the same number of views of your book, you will sell more copies of it.

I'm sure you've heard that it's songs played on the radio that become hits and not the other way around (like you'd think it would be). Well, something similar happens with Amazon – but unlike in the music industry, you don't have to pay for it or do anybody any little favors.

Being a bestseller will help you sell more books, and vice versa.

What do you need to become a bestseller in an Amazon category?

First of all, it's fundamental that you properly understand what the **ABSR** is. This number (which we already used in the previous chapter to find the most lucrative keywords) depends on the sales and/or downloads of a book over a given time period, compared to other books on Amazon The more sales/downloads, the lower the ABSR.

Let's imagine that, at a certain point, your book has an ABSR of 100. This means that there are only 99 other books on all of Amazon that are selling more than yours. If your ABSR was 1000, there would currently be 999 books selling better than yours, and so on and so forth.

So, if you have the lowest ABSR of all the books in a given category, you would be nº1 in that category. It's that simple.

Example: if you choose a category where the nº1 has an ABSR of 500, then to reach first place, your book will need an ABSR of 499 or less.

This means that the categories you choose when uploading your book to KDP have a direct impact on your chancing of becoming a bestselling author.

How to find the best categories.

To find the most suitable categories with the most potential for turning your work into a bestseller, just follow three simple steps:

1. Find the possible categories for your book.

To find these possible categories, head to the "Product details" section of similar books to yours (they may be in direct competition with you or not) and note down the categories these appear under. You'll see that each book is included in two or three different categories.

Location of categories under "Product details".

Try to make a list of at least 5 possible categories.

2. Find out the n°1 book in each category.

Now that you have your list of possible categories, it's time to find out which have the best chance of turning your book into a bestseller.

To do this, first go to the list of the bestselling books in each of these categories by clicking on the name of each category in the "Product details" section of each book you're researching.

Once you're in, click on the n°1 book for each of these categories and note down its ABSR. This is the ABSR you'll have to beat in order to become a bestseller in that category. The higher the ABSR, the easier you'll find it to reach n°1.

Pro tip: If you use Publisher Rocket, then in addition to saving yourself hours of work, you can find out the number of books you need to sell in twenty-four hours in order to reach first place in each category.

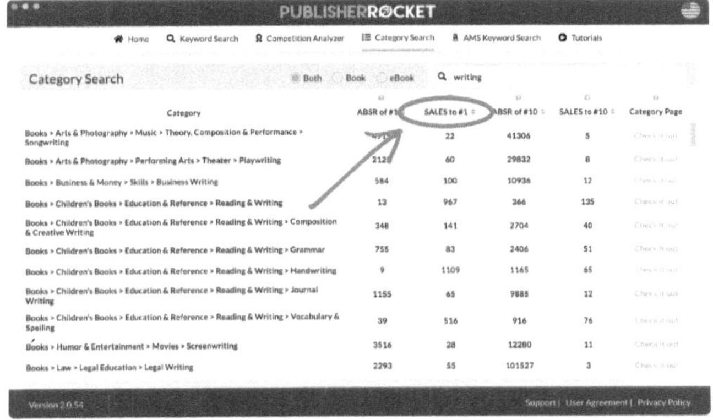

Category	ABSR of #1	SALES to #1	ABSR of #10	SALES to #10	Category Page
Books > Arts & Photography > Music > Theory, Composition & Performance > Songwriting		22	41306	5	Check it out
Books > Arts & Photography > Performing Arts > Theater > Playwriting	2125	60	29832	8	Check it out
Books > Business & Money > Skills > Business Writing	584	100	10936	12	Check it out
Books > Children's Books > Education & Reference > Reading & Writing	13	967	366	135	Check it out
Books > Children's Books > Education & Reference > Reading & Writing > Composition & Creative Writing	348	141	2704	40	Check it out
Books > Children's Books > Education & Reference > Reading & Writing > Grammar	755	83	2406	51	Check it out
Books > Children's Books > Education & Reference > Reading & Writing > Handwriting	9	1109	1165	65	Check it out
Books > Children's Books > Education & Reference > Reading & Writing > Journal Writing	1155	65	9885	12	Check it out
Books > Children's Books > Education & Reference > Reading & Writing > Vocabulary & Spelling	39	516	916	76	Check it out
Books > Humor & Entertainment > Movies > Screenwriting	3516	28	12280	11	Check it out
Books > Law > Legal Education > Legal Writing	2293	55	101527	3	Check it out

Version 2.0.54   Support | User Agreement | Privacy Policy

And that's it. With this small research you've just conducted, you now know which categories are the most suitable for your book's topic and, most importantly, which ones have the best chances of boosting you to become a bestseller author: those with a higher ABSR.

Now you just need to choose your three favorites and add them in the appropriate section when you upload your book to KDP.

STEP 7

Pricing:
Strategies and promotions

You're almost there. The last section you will have to fill out when uploading your book to KDP is your book's price. Because unlike what happens when you work through a publishing house, on Amazon the price is set by you.

Is this a good thing? Very.

But before moving onto the technical aspects of this, let me tell you a story:

My cousin once asked me if I could meet with a friend of his who was a neurosurgeon and writer. He told me that he had published his first book through a publishing house, but he was planning to publish his second through Amazon and didn't know whether to do it or whether it was a good idea. Of course, I told him I was happy to have a coffee with him and help him as much as I could.

A few days later, he called me and we met at one of my favorite cafes (the kind I write in). To my surprise, I had taken more time learning about him and his book than he had about me.

The first thing he said to me when we sat down was: "so, your cousin tells me you have a book on Amazon". Things weren't looking good.

He admitted to me – although I already knew it – that his book actually hadn't been published through a publishing house, but rather he had spent over $7000 on the *printing scam*, and only sold around a hundred copies. This is the only reason he had wanted to talk to me: my cousin had told him I had published "safely", without spending a lot of money, and he was going to publish his new book himself whatever it took (although he couldn't imagine making any profit from it) and wanted to know if it was possible to save a few bucks.

Based on this, where the only thing this person knew about me was that I had published through Amazon without investing much, my recommendations weren't very useful – in his eyes, I had no authority. It was more like a meeting between two friends defending their respective points of view than it was a free advice session. Fun, sure, but not awfully valuable.

In the end, I decided to relax and enjoy my coffee while having a chat with an interesting person. I wasn't there to prove myself, and my ego was perfectly comfortable. However, not long before we said goodbye, the topic of pricing came up and things changed. When we had already asked for the check, he suddenly asked me:

- Just out of interest, how much are you selling your book for?
- Well, right now, the Kindle version is at $10, and the paperback at $30.
- What?! $30?! How many pages is your book?!
- Around 170, if I remember correctly.
- Listen, let me tell you something: my book has over 400 pages and I'm selling it at $14.99, and I've barely sold a hundred copies in over three years. At your prices, you're not going to sell at all.

It's true that I wasn't there to prove anything to anyone, but since the topic had come up... telling him about my sales was highly satisfying :)

His expression was incredulous, and he began to debate (mostly with himself) and explain "to me" why "I" couldn't be selling that many books while simultaneously asking me how I had managed it (?!).

This neurosurgeon-slash-writer was trying nervously to tell me that a book is sold by weight (no doubt that's what the "publishing house" told him), so mine "needed" to be a lot cheaper if I wanted to sell it.

I tried to explain the **concept of value** to him in a few different ways, but there was no telling him. Eventually, I took a napkin from the dispenser (the kind you need twenty-three of to get your hands clean), pretended I was writing something on it, folded it up and slid it across the table, telling him:

- Imagine that on this napkin is written the formula that enables you to turn water into gold. How much would you pay me for it?

- Everything I had (he answered pretty quickly).
- Would you pay me $30?
- I'd give you my house for it.
- But this napkin barely weighs anything.

I don't think he liked my napkin metaphor much, but it got my point across, because the next thing he said was "for $30, you're not going to sell many books", before paying the check at the counter, saying goodbye, and never contacting me again.

Am I telling you this story so that you set any price for your book that you like, no matter what the rest of the market is doing?

No.

I just want you to understand that the price you set for your book needs to have a reason behind it, and that – especially if we're talking about a non-fiction book – it shouldn't be based on its weight.

How to price your book.

Just like with the writing process itself, setting a price for your work is half art, half science. The aspects to bear in mind when finding the perfect amount are myriad, but let's look at what I consider to be the **3 most important**:

1. Your objectives.

The first step to finding the right price is to ask yourself what the objective of your book is:

a) You may see your book as an investment or mini-business in itself, and want to get the most profits possible from sales – in which case, you're looking at finding the best price/sales/income relationship.

That means, generally and logically speaking, the higher the price, the fewer sales, and the lower the price the more sales. This is clear, but what price/sales relationship will give us the most income at the end of each month?

b) Alternatively, you may see your book as a way to get your message across and help as many people as you can, without minding what profit you make from selling it. If this is you, it's logical that the cheaper your book is, the more people you'll be able to reach.

WARNING: Someone who buys your book just because it's cheap, as an impulse buy, may not end up reading it. In addition, a low price can suggest low quality, which could be reflected in your reviews and negatively impact on your sales in the long term.

c) It's likely that your objective for your book is somewhere in between. You may want to reach as many people as possible without caring about profits from direct sales of your book... but you're also hoping to get some profits, or to use your book as a way to get customers to buy other products or services from you later. You may want to use your book as a kind of resumé to get a new job, or a promotion at your current company. The possibilities are endless; **what matters is that you're clear on your objective**.

2. The competition.

Taking a look at your competition is the fastest way to get an idea of the prices other books in your category sell for. This is a great starting point to avoid aiming too high or too low.

But don't get obsessed with this, either. It's just a reference point. I have had customers terrified to set the same price as well-known authors or books with many more pages than their own, and ending up setting their prices purely based on this criterion, with no real strategy in mind. **You have to get rid of that fear**.

Amazon has democratized both publishing and selling books: not only can you publish your book just the same as your favorite authors... you can get ahead of them and beat their sales figures!

Unlike what has always happened in traditional bookshops, where the best spot (the shiny, well-lit shelf just in front of the entrance, packed from top to bottom with copies of the same book) was reserved for the big author that a big publishing house decided to promote that month, with Amazon that spot is just the first in the list when a reader searches for something (whether through keywords or by category) and **it's reserved for... the best book**. Not for the best-known author, or the publishing house that paid to be there. If your book is the best, it doesn't matter if it's the first time you've ever published anything, or if you're not even a household name in your own house – **it will appear at the top of the list**. In everyone's eyeline.

And how do Amazon decide who is the best? It's simple: **with stars**. This is how Amazon readers show their satisfaction rating. The more stars, the happier they are, with five being the maximum.

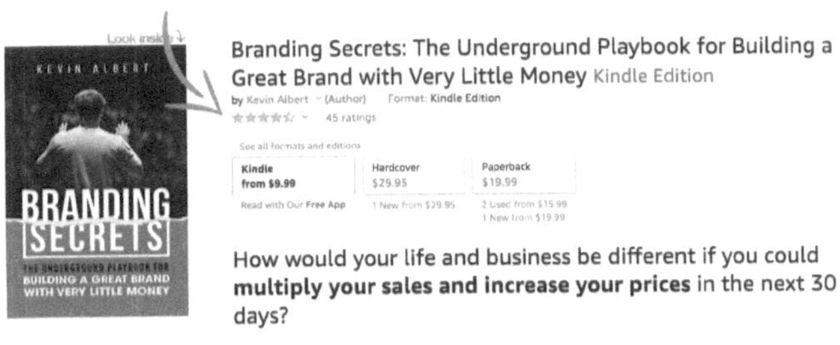

Location of the star rating on the product page.

This will also work in your favor as a new author in terms of expectations. When we watch a movie we have high expectations for, because it contains our favorite actor, for example, it's easier for us to be disappointed. However, the first time we "risk" investing our money in a movie or book by an unknown writer, we have no expectations yet and it's less likely we'll be disappointed. On top of that, readers seem to be more permissive in terms of print quality or minor grammatical errors, for example, with self-published authors than with big publishing houses, from whom they demand near perfection.

If you're still worried about pricing your book the same as "big name writers", remember that I didn't set the price of my first book the same as the competition – I set it at exactly double! $10 for the Kindle version, $30 for the paperback.

While risky, there was a reason for this strategy. Firstly, I wanted to differentiate myself, as a book by an unknown author that's double the price of books by well-known author will inevitably make readers wonder: "what the hell is up with this book?" (This is why it's important to have good reviews). Secondly, I knew my book was worthwhile in comparison with other branding books on the market, which seem only to talk about companies the size of Coca-Cola.

Careful! If you decide to set a higher price than your competition in order to increase your book's perceived value, make sure its real value doesn't disappoint your readers.

In any case, the most-used strategy in relation to the competition's prices, which will also help you sleep at night (I think I like danger too much), is to launch your book at a lower price and then increase it to match the competition when you reach a certain number of reasonable reviews (at least half those of the competition).

3. The value you add.

As I explained to my cousin's friend, when it comes to pricing your book, one factor you should bear in mind – especially for non-fiction – is the value it adds for readers.

Logic, and Amazon statistics, indicate that we are prepared to pay more money for a non-fiction book than a fiction one. In other words: we will pay more to solve a problem than we will to be entertained.

So, before you set a price for your book, ask yourself: "what can my book do for my readers? Are there any other books on the market that do the same thing?". I don't mean that your book has to present a completely original solution or idea. Sometimes, saying the same thing from a different perspective or with a better structure can in itself be priceless.

So, does this mean that if your book solves some existential problem, you can set whatever price you want for it? No. What it means is that you can set a "high" price in relation to your competition.

Although I would happily pay over a thousand dollars for some of the books on my own shelf (they've earned me a lot more than that), if you really want to sell, you need to set a "book price". As high as you want, but appropriate for a book.

Even if you know the secret to eating without getting fat – something millions of people would give their right arm for – the price of your book needs to meet the expected standards. My recommendation in this case would probably be to use your work to position yourself as an expert and obtain clients for personal consulting or one of your conferences later on – then, you really can charge as much as you want. It's sad that it has to be that way, but it's what we're used to.

I have been invited to conferences costing over $3000 and never learned anything more than I already knew from the book by the author giving the talk, which cost less than $30.

Psychological strategies.

Now, let's look at two simple psychological and logical strategies that will help you sell more books.

a) The magic of the .99

Like it or not, this crude strategy invented in the 19th century still has a significant impact on our shopping habits.

If you price your book at $5, for example, you'll sell fewer than if you set it at $4.99. It's that simple. From a logical point of view, this makes no sense: $4.99 is only one cent less than $5, which doesn't constitute any savings for the buyer. But our brains interpret it differently.

Since we read from left to right, our brain – which loves to simplify things – focuses on the number before the dot. This means that when the price starts with a 4, our brain files it under "4" (4 dollars and something), but if the price starts with a 5, we file it under "5".

Another hypothesis says that prices that end in .99 are associated with discounts or promotions. And when we think we're getting a deal, we're more likely to buy it right away.

Pro tip: when you've finally decided on a price for your book and you enter it into the corresponding field on KDP, don't make the mistake of letting the platform calculate the same price for the rest of your markets as your main market (which you choose). If, for example, you decided to use the .99 strategy, apply it manually to all available markets. It will take you less than a minute and make a big difference over the course of a year.

b) Multiprices.

If you have written, or plan to write, more than one book, you may think it's a good idea to set the same price for all of them (the price that worked best for you elsewhere) – especially if they have the same theme and similar lengths. This will end up having a negative impact on your sales.

Using what's known as multiple pricing will help you benefit from different customers' **value perception**. For example, if you price one book at \$11.99 and another at \$19.99, thanks to the price comparison that happens subconsciously in consumers' heads, you will attract both readers looking for a good deal and readers who prefer the premium option.

Experiment.

One of the good things about Amazon is that you can change the price of your book whenever you want, as often as you want.

You can start by pricing your work following the recommendations I've given you in this chapter, or you can do the total opposite and ignore my tips entirely. In the end, there is no perfect price, and no matter what I tell you or how many successful cases I show you, nothing can replace the power of experimentation.

Are you someone who thinks the price of your book should be based on the number of pages or words it has? Go ahead. Amazon itself will show you price tables according to this criterion.

Have you read somewhere that the eBook should cost half the physical version? Try it out.

Or do you think that if you price them similarly, then sales of your paperback will go through the roof? Give it a go and see what happens.

Allow yourself to try things, and don't be afraid of making mistakes. Worst case scenario, you'll have a month of slower sales (or profits), and the next month[11] you can try a different combination of prices (Kindle and paperback) that worked well for you before, or try something totally new.

Can I tell you a secret? I realized that every time I make a small modification on KDP, whether it's to fix an error in the description, upload a new cover, or change the price of one of my books, my sales go up that week. Don't ask me why, but **Amazon's algorithm likes change**. If that doesn't encourage you to experiment, I don't know what will.

---

[11] I recommend that each test lasts at least 30 days so you can draw solid conclusions from it.

Promotions.

Signing up to the KDP program will enable you to run two kinds of promotion on your book, totally free: **Kindle Countdown Deals,** and **free book promotions**.

To start a promotion, just click "promote and advertise" from your KDP dashboard, and once you're in, select one of the above two options.

Run a Price Promotion

Sign your book up for a Kindle Countdown Deal or a Free Book Promotion. Only one promotion can be enabled per enrollment period.

◉ Kindle Countdown Deal Learn more
◯ Free Book Promotion Learn more

Create a new Kindle Countdown Deal

KDP Select promotion options.

1. Kindle Countdown Deals.

This type of promotion will allow you to set a lower price for your book for a limited period. Customers will be able to see its usual price alongside the promotional price on the book details page, as well as a clock showing the time remaining at the promotional price.

All you have to do is select a **start** and **finish date** (with a maximum period of seven days), the **number of price increases** (with a maximum of five) and the **starting price**.

Imagine you have a Kindle book with a normal price of $9.99 and you decide to run this promotion from Monday to Friday, with a starting price of $1.99. With this configuration, Amazon will show your book at $1.99 for 37 hours and at $5.99 for the remaining 38 hours, before returning it to its original price of $9.99.

Increments		Duration	Price	% Discount
1	21 junio 2020 at 8:00 (PDT)	37h	$1.99	81%
2	22 junio 2020 at 21:00 (PDT)	37h	$3.99	61%
3	24 junio 2020 at 10:00 (PDT)	38h	$5.99	41%
Fin	26 junio 2020 at 0:00 (PDT)		$9.99	

Example of a configuration with Kindle Countdown Deals.

The idea is to motivate people to buy with the incentive that, if they leave it till later, the book will be more expensive. The bigger the discount, the more motivating it is.

This type of promotion has **two main advantages**:

- **You maintain your royalties.** You will receive royalties according to your normal rate, applied to the promotional price. So, if you're signed up to the 70% royalties option, you'll get 70% even if the price is less than $2.99.
- **More sales,** both because of the incentive of seeing a reduced price and a countdown timer, and because of the greater visibility

you will get by including your book in an additional category: "Featured Kindle Countdown Deals".

Requirements for participating in Kindle Countdown Deals:

- The eBook must be signed up to KDP Select for at least 30 days before you launch the promotion.
- The price must have remained the same for those 30 days, and for 14 days following the end of the promotion.
- The minimum discount is $1 on Amazon.com and £1 on *Amazon.co.uk* (the only two markets on which you can run this promotion currently).
- However long you set the time period for, this will count as a complete promotion (you can't divide the promotion between separate time periods).
- You haven't run another KDP Select promotion for that eBook. You can only

schedule one promotion (free book or Kindle Countdown Deals) per inscription period with KDP Select (90 days).

- Kindle Countdown Deals must be scheduled at least 24 hours before their start date. For example, for the promotion to begin on January 10th, you can schedule it at any point prior to January 8th.

- The Kindle Countdown Deals promotion will end a maximum of 14 days before your KDP Select sign-up period ends. If you renew your book with KDP Select for another 90 days, your Kindle Countdown Deals promotion can end on the last day of your current period with KDP Select.

2. Free book promotions.

This type of promotion enables you to offer your book for free for 5 days (consecutive or alternating) for each sign-up period with KDP Select (90 days). And, unlike Kindle Countdown

Deals, **it is not limited** to Amazon.com and Amazon.co.uk.

The best thing to do if you decide to use this promotion is to run the 5 days consecutively, starting on Sunday and ending on Thursday, since these are the days of the week with the most sales.

A few years ago, this promotion gave great results because during the days for which people could get the book for free, you would get a lot of downloads (especially if used in conjunction with other strategies), which sent your book up the **free books ranking.** When the promotional period was over, the rank you achieved on this list would help you move up the **paid books ranking** (the one we're interested in). Nowadays, you don't get this transfer of positions between the two lists, so this option is used less widely – although it can still be helpful in certain specific cases:

- Authors publishing a book for the first time, with no established target market. This can be a good way to get a significant number of downloads and make yourself known, as well as obtaining some early reviews.

- Authors who aren't looking to make money from their book. A free book will, without a doubt, be downloaded by more people. But be careful – more downloads doesn't necessarily mean more readers. People who only download a book because it's free tend to accumulate hundreds of books they never get round to reading.

- Authors planning to turn their books into series. It can be a good idea to offer the first book for free as a hook to get more sales on your other books later. This wouldn't have happened to you with the first book in this series, would it? Sorry :)

Upload your book to Amazon

If you've followed the 7 steps in this book, you have all the elements you need ready to upload your book to KDP.

To begin, all you need to do is create an account. Go to _kdp.amazon.com,_ click "Sign in" and enter your Amazon details, or click "Sign up" and create a new account. Fill in your personal and financial details and tell them the bank account you want Amazon to pay your royalties into (it's much better than getting a check).

All that's left is to upload your book. Choose the format you want to start with —Kindle, Paperback or Hardcover— and check the corresponding box.

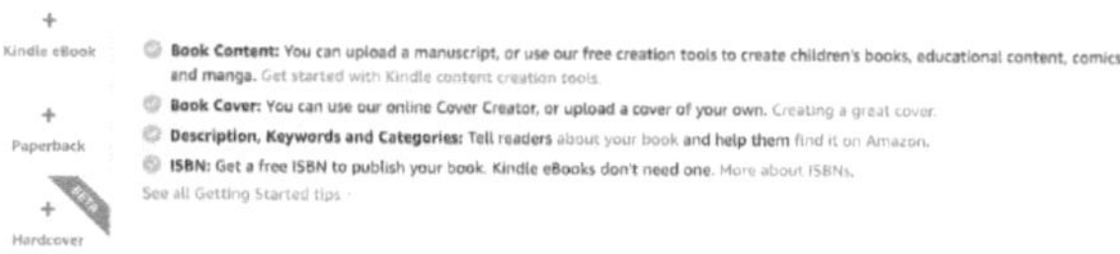

KDP user panel.

You'll see that the details to fill in are classed into three main sections: details, content and book price. It's all very simple. There are only five things that tend to generate doubts the first time you upload a book (if you have any others, don't hesitate to ask me):

1. **Publishing rights**. Check the first option: «I own the copyright and I hold the necessary publishing rights».

2. **Physical ISBN**. Click «Assign me a free KDP ISBN».

3. **Territories**. Select «All territories».

4. **Digital Rights Management (DRM).** I recommend you don't enable this, as it's been proven that books with DRM don't sell as well.

5. **Signing up to KDP Select.** Of course, I recommend signing up, since – as I mentioned before – it's given me better results in my experiments (more profits), but it's ultimately a personal decision.

And that's it!

You will have realized by now that, as I said at the start of this book, self-publishing a book on Amazon (uploading it to KDP) takes no more than thirty minutes, but self-publishing a book on Amazon **properly and with the best chances of success** requires a little more preparation in order to correctly organize each of the sections we've gone through.

I hope I've conveyed the importance of taking care over each of these 7 steps and that I have explained them clearly and simply, so that you too can achieve, without needing a publishing house...

Successful self-publishing!

So, what's next?

First of all...

Congratulations on making it this far!

Not many people write a book during their lives, but even fewer take the necessary time and interest in making this legacy reach the hands of their readers with the quality it merits.

You didn't fall for the printing scam, you decided not to rely on what a publishing house says, and you managed to self-publish your book without it looking self-published: all this is something to be very proud of.

If you followed all the steps in this guide, you will have achieved:

- Professional editing at amateur prices by using marketplaces.
- Formatting your book as well as, or better than, any publishing house by using templates.
- Designing and validating your book cover by choosing from over a hundred different proposals.
- Boost your book sales thanks to a thorough keyword search.
- Multiplied your chances of becoming a bestselling author by correctly choosing your categories.
- And so on.

So now what?

If you have written and published your book by following the recommendations in Successful Self-Publishing 1 and 2, all that's left is to follow one last indispensable step before you can proudly proclaim that you are a **professional writer** and that your books aren't just your hobby: **selling them!**

- Would you like your book to become a **bestseller in under 24 hours**?
- Do you want to **turn your bestseller into a longseller**?
- Why are reviews the key to a book's success or failure?
- Do you want to know how to get reviews Amazon?
- Is it possible to **retire on just one book... and in less than a year**?
- Do you want to **guarantee $700 a month** through book sales?
- Would you like to get your book translated for free?
- ...

The answers to all these questions, and many more, can be found in the third and final instalment of Successful Self-publishing: **How to sell a book on Amazon… and live off it!**

soykevinalbert.com/books/ssp3

Whether you want to live off your book(s) or you're just looking to share your message with as many people as you can, **you need to learn how to sell your book.**

Important

In order for my book to help other readers like you, **your opinion is very important**. I would appreciate it greatly if you could **leave me a review** on your favorite platform to tell me what you thought of my book so that I can keep on improving it:

- Is there anything you felt was missing?
- Is there anything you would add or remove?
- ...

If, for some reason, you thought my book was a pile of trash, please email me and I will give you back 100% of your money for having wasted your time, and/or I will resolve any doubts you might still have.

The main factor that drives me to keep writing is helping people, so if I'm not doing that, I'll happily do something else instead.

Best of luck, fellow writer!
Kevin Albert

A gift just for you!

Would you like to **read my next book completely FREE**? Scan the code below and **join my readers' club**!

Great surprises await you: be the first to read my new releases, listen to my audiobooks for free, get signed and personalized copies... and so much more!

Other books by Kevin Albert